Sheila Hancock

Sheila Hancock is a British actress and author. She was born on February 22, 1933, in Blackgang, Isle of Wight, England. Over the course of her career, she has appeared in various film, television, and stage productions, earning critical acclaim for her work.

Hancock began her acting career in the 1950s and gained recognition for her stage performances, including her role in the West End production of "Rattle of a Simple Man" in 1962. She also appeared in several British films, such as "The Anniversary" (1968) and "Carry On Cleo" (1964).

In the 1970s, Sheila Hancock transitioned to television and became a familiar face on British screens. She starred in the sitcom "The Rag Trade" and played the lead role in the popular drama series "The Bed-Sit Girl." Hancock also appeared in other television shows, including "Doctor Who" and "EastEnders."

Throughout her career, Hancock has worked extensively in the theater, performing in both classic and contemporary plays. She has received critical acclaim for her performances in plays such as "The Winter's Tale," "Sweeney Todd," and "Sister Act."

In addition to her acting career, Sheila Hancock is an accomplished author. She has written several books, including her memoir "The Two of Us," which chronicles her marriage to actor John Thaw, and "Just Me," a memoir about her life after Thaw's death.

Sheila Hancock has been recognized for her contributions to the arts and entertainment industry. She was appointed Commander of the Order of the British Empire (CBE) in 2011 for her services to drama, and she received a Lifetime Achievement Award at the 2018 Women in Film and TV Awards.

In the late 1990s and early 2000s, Sheila Hancock appeared in several successful television dramas, including "The Russian Bride," "The Russian Bride Returns," and "Murder Most Horrid." Her portrayal of characters with depth and complexity earned her critical acclaim.

Hancock's talent as a stage actress remained prominent throughout her career. In 2006, she starred in the West End revival of the musical "Cabaret," playing the role of Fraulein Schneider. Her performance garnered positive reviews and showcased her versatility as an actress.

Sheila Hancock's television work continued to flourish in the 2010s. She appeared in the BBC drama series "New Tricks" from 2013 to 2015, portraying the character Germaine Simpson. Her performance in the series was widely praised by audiences and critics alike.

In addition to her acting achievements, Hancock has also been involved in charitable and humanitarian efforts. She has actively supported various causes, including organizations working for cancer research and the welfare of older people.

Throughout her career, Sheila Hancock has received numerous awards and accolades for her contributions to the arts. In 2018, she was honored with a Special Award at the BAFTA Television Awards for her outstanding career in television and her commitment to the industry.

It's important to note that the entertainment industry is dynamic, and actors often continue to take on new projects. Therefore, for the most recent information on Sheila Hancock's career and endeavors, I recommend checking reliable sources such as news outlets and her official social media accounts.

However, based on her accomplished career and dedication to the arts, it is likely that Sheila Hancock has continued to pursue her passion for acting and writing. She has demonstrated a remarkable versatility and talent throughout her career, successfully transitioning between stage, film, and television.

Hancock's contributions to the entertainment industry have left a lasting impact, and she is regarded as a respected figure within the British acting community. Her memorable performances, both comedic and dramatic, have captivated audiences over the years.

In addition to her artistic achievements, Sheila Hancock has also shared her personal experiences and insights through her writing. Her memoirs, such as "The Two of Us" and "Just Me," have allowed readers to gain a deeper understanding of her life and career.

As a prominent figure in the arts, Sheila Hancock's legacy continues to inspire aspiring actors and actresses, and her contributions to the industry are appreciated by fans and fellow professionals alike.

For the latest updates on Sheila Hancock's career and recent projects, I recommend referring to reliable sources such as news outlets, official social media accounts, or her official website.

Therefore, I cannot provide any further information about Sheila Hancock's career beyond what I have already shared. To stay up to date with her recent activities, I recommend checking reliable sources such as news outlets, entertainment websites, or Sheila Hancock's official social media accounts. These sources will provide the most accurate and timely information about her ongoing projects and achievements.

Sheila Hancock's contributions to the entertainment industry, both on stage and screen, have left an indelible mark. Her talent, versatility, and dedication to her craft have garnered her widespread acclaim throughout her career. She has inspired audiences with her performances and has been recognized with prestigious awards and honors for her outstanding contributions to the arts.

Throughout her life, Sheila Hancock has not only excelled as an actress but also demonstrated her abilities as an author, sharing her personal experiences and insights through her memoirs. Her writing has allowed readers to gain a deeper understanding of her life, career, and the challenges she has faced.

Sheila Hancock's impact as an artist and her passion for storytelling have touched the lives of many. Her work continues to inspire both fellow actors and fans alike, and she remains an influential figure within the British entertainment industry.

For the most up-to-date and accurate information about Sheila Hancock's career, recent projects, and achievements, please refer to reliable sources.

Early life

Sheila Cameron Hancock was born in Blackgang on the Isle of Wight. Her parents were Enrico Cameron Hancock and Ivy Louise Hancock (née Woodward). Enrico had a background working for Thomas Cook and grew up in Milan before working for Vickers. He later worked as a publican and hotel manager for Brakspear Brewery in various locations, including the Isle of Wight, Berkshire, and King's Cross, London.

Ivy Hancock worked at Hedley Mitchells, a department store in Erith, where she set up a café and theatre booking office. Prior to that, she worked in gloves and lingerie and had experience working with her husband in pubs and hotels. Before her marriage, Ivy had worked at a pub in Lewisham and a flower shop in Greenwich.

In 1938, after leaving the hospitality industry, the Hancock family moved to a semi-detached house in Latham Road, Bexleyheath. Sheila considered this move to be "dreadfully dull" compared to the bustling environment of King's Cross. The relocation marked a change in their social status, as they transitioned from working-class to lower-middle-class. Sheila had an older sister named Billie, who was seven years her senior.

Sheila Hancock received her education at various schools. She attended St Etheldreda's Convent at Ely Place in Holborn, followed by Upton Road Junior School and Upland Junior School. During World War II, she was evacuated to Wallingford, Oxfordshire (then in Berkshire) and Crewkerne, Somerset. After the war, Hancock attended Dartford County Grammar School and later went on to study at the Royal Academy of Dramatic Art (RADA).

The early years of Sheila Hancock's life provided a diverse backdrop and experiences that would shape her future career as an actress.

Theatre

Sheila Hancock's career in the theater spans several decades, and she has appeared in a wide range of productions, both in the West End and with renowned theater companies.

During the 1950s, Hancock worked in repertory theater before making her West End debut in 1958, replacing Joan Sims in the play "Breath of Spring." She continued to make her mark in the West End, appearing in productions such as Joan Littlewood's Theatre Workshop production of "Make Me An Offer" in 1959. In 1961, she appeared in Peter Cook's revue "One Over the Eight" alongside Kenneth Williams, and in 1962, she starred in "Rattle of a Simple Man."

Hancock also made her Broadway debut in 1965, appearing in the play "Entertaining Mr Sloane." She later took on notable roles in musicals, including playing Miss Hannigan in the original London cast of "Annie" in 1978 and Mrs Lovett in the original London production of "Sweeney Todd" at the Theatre Royal, Drury Lane in 1980.

Sheila Hancock has also worked extensively with prestigious theater companies. She appeared in productions for the Royal Shakespeare Company (RSC), including "The Winter's Tale," "Titus Andronicus," and "A Delicate Balance." At the National Theatre, she performed in Neil Bartlett's "In Extremis/De Profundis," "The Cherry Orchard," and "The Duchess of Malfi." Hancock holds the distinction of being the first woman to direct the RSC touring company, directing "A Midsummer Night's Dream." She was also the first woman to direct in the Olivier Theatre at the National Theatre, helming "The Critic." Additionally, she served as associate artistic director of the Cambridge Theatre Company.

In 2006, Hancock received critical acclaim and awards for her portrayal of Fräulein Schneider in the West End revival of the musical "Cabaret" at the Lyric Theatre. She won the Laurence Olivier Award and the Clarence Derwent Award for Best Performance in a Supporting Role in a Musical. She continued to take on prominent roles, such as playing Mother Superior in "Sister Act the Musical" at the London Palladium in 2009, for which she was nominated for an Olivier Award.

In subsequent years, Hancock starred in various productions, including the comedy "Barking in Essex" in 2013, the UK premiere of the musical "Grey Gardens" in 2016, and the play "Harold and Maude" in 2018. In 2019, she starred in the musical "This Is My Family" at the Minerva Theatre in Chichester.

Sheila Hancock's theatrical career exemplifies her versatility and talent as she has taken on diverse roles in both plays and musicals, receiving critical acclaim and awards for her performances.

Television

Sheila Hancock has had a prolific career in television, with numerous roles spanning various genres. Her first notable television role was as Carol in the BBC sitcom "The Rag Trade" in the early 1960s. She went on to star in several other sitcoms, including "The Bed-Sit Girl," "Mr Digby Darling," and "Now Take My Wife."

Hancock's television credits include appearances in popular shows such as "Doctor Who," where she portrayed a parody of Margaret Thatcher in the episode "The Happiness Patrol." She also appeared in "Kavanagh QC" alongside her husband, John Thaw, as well as shows like "Gone to the Dogs," "Brighton Belles," "EastEnders," "The Russian Bride," "Bedtime," "Fortysomething," "Feather Boy," "Bleak House," "New Tricks," "Hustle," and "The Catherine Tate Show."

In 2008, Hancock played the role of a terminally ill patient seeking assisted suicide in one of "The Last Word" monologues, a series of dramatic monologues for the BBC written specifically for her by Hugo Blick. She also appeared in the BBC anthology series "Moving On" in the episode "The Rain Has Stopped."

Aside from acting, Hancock has presented several documentaries. In 2010, she presented "Suffragette City" as part of the BBC series "A History of the World," exploring the suffragette movement through objects from the Museum of London's collection. In 2011, she presented "Sheila Hancock Brushes Up: The Art of Watercolours," delving into the history of watercolour art. She also presented the ITV Perspectives documentary "Sheila Hancock – The Brilliant Brontë Sisters" in 2013, examining the lives and works of the Brontë sisters.

Hancock has made notable guest appearances in various shows, including a Christmas special of "Strictly Come Dancing" in 2012 and an episode of the medical drama "Casualty" for its 30th anniversary in 2016. She appeared in the Sky One comedy-drama series "Delicious" alongside Dawn French, Emilia Fox, and Iain Glen from 2016 to 2019. Hancock also made a guest appearance in an episode of the Inspector Morse prequel series "Endeavour" in 2017, alongside her stepdaughter Abigail Thaw.

In recent years, Hancock co-presented the Channel 4 series "Great Canal Journeys" with Gyles Brandreth, and she appeared in the Sky One fantasy drama "A Discovery of Witches" as Goody Alsop. She also had a role as Eileen in ITV's "Unforgotten" in 2021.

Sheila Hancock's extensive television career demonstrates her versatility and talent across a wide range of roles and genres.

Other work

In addition to her work in theater and television, Sheila Hancock has had various other ventures and achievements throughout her career.

In 1963, Hancock released a comedy single titled "My Last Cigarette." The song humorously depicts someone attempting to quit smoking but succumbing to the temptation of "just one more cigarette."

She also appeared in the film "The Wildcats of St Trinian's" in 1980, although she has expressed her dissatisfaction with the movie, referring to it as "one of the worst films ever made."

Hancock has had a significant presence in radio. She has been a regular participant on the BBC Radio 4 panel game "Just a Minute" since 1967. She starred in the BBC Radio 2 comedy series "Thank You, Mrs Fothergill" in 1978-79, alongside Pat Coombs. In 1995, Hancock provided the voice of Granny Weatherwax in BBC Radio 4's adaptation of Terry Pratchett's Discworld novel "Wyrd Sisters." She also appeared in the BBC Radio 4 series "North by Northamptonshire" in 2011, alongside Geoffrey Palmer.

Sheila Hancock has made guest appearances on various television shows, including "Grumpy Old Women," "Room 101," "Have I Got News for You," and "Would I Lie To You?". In 2010, she served as a judge on the BBC show "Over the Rainbow" alongside Charlotte Church, Andrew Lloyd Webber, and John Partridge.

From 2007 to 2012, Hancock held the position of Chancellor of the University of Portsmouth, demonstrating her commitment to education and the arts.

Hancock also had the honor of being the subject of the television program "This Is Your Life" in 1977. She was surprised by Eamonn Andrews during the curtain call of the play "The Bed Before Yesterday" at the Lyric Theatre in London.

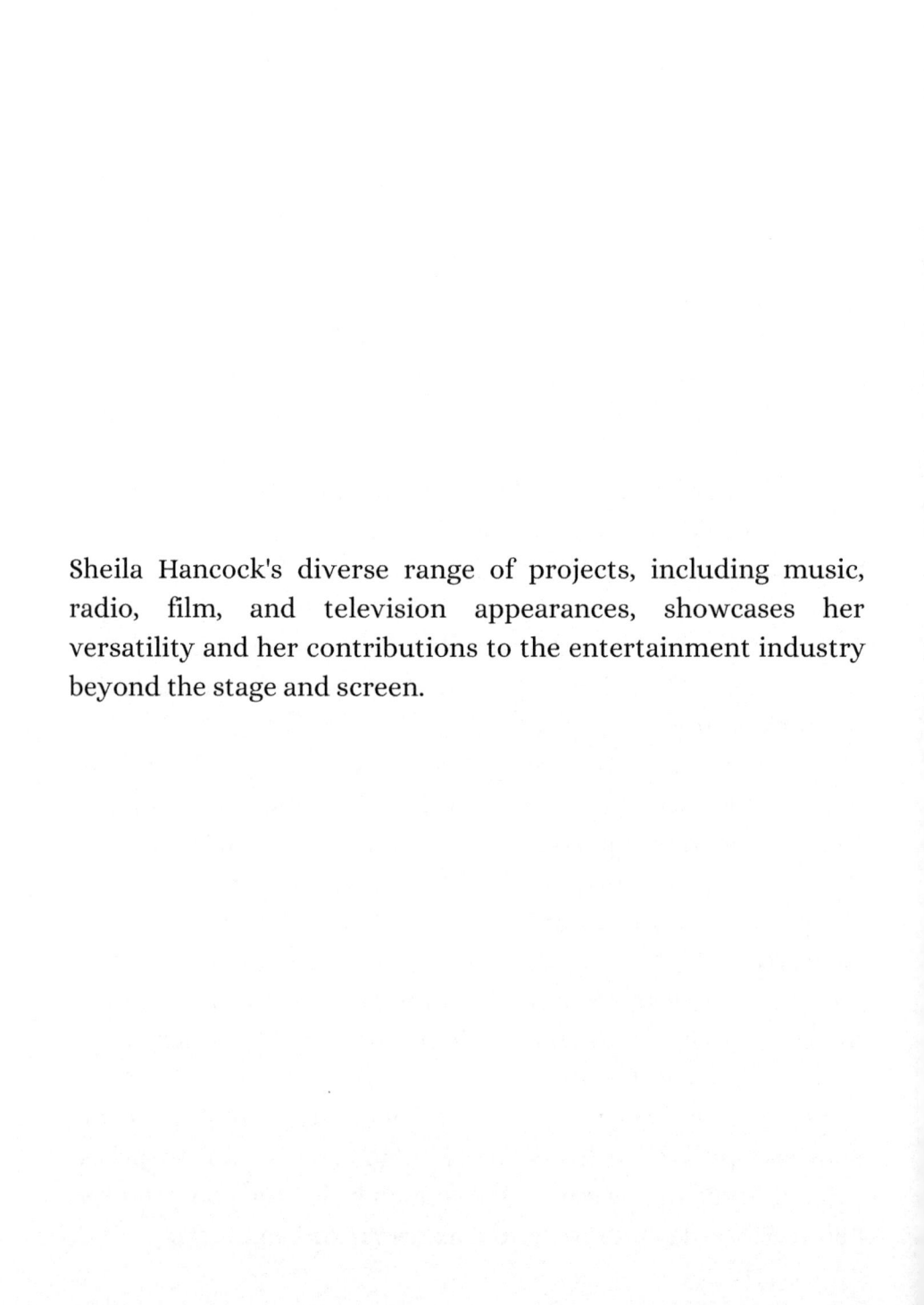

Sheila Hancock's diverse range of projects, including music, radio, film, and television appearances, showcases her versatility and her contributions to the entertainment industry beyond the stage and screen.

Personal life

Sheila Hancock's personal life has been marked by marriages, family, and personal challenges. She was first married to actor Alec Ross from 1955 until his death in 1971. They had a daughter named Melanie, born in 1964. In 1973, Hancock married actor John Thaw, known for his role as Inspector Morse. Thaw adopted Melanie, and they also had another daughter named Joanna. Thaw had a daughter named Abigail from his previous marriage, who became part of their blended family. All three daughters have followed in their parents' footsteps and become actresses.

Hancock and Thaw remained married until his death from oesophageal cancer in 2002. Hancock herself was diagnosed with breast cancer in 1988 but made a full recovery. She wrote about her marriage to Thaw and their lives together in her 2004 book "The Two of Us," which serves as a dual biography. She later published "Just Me" in 2008, an autobiographical account of coming to terms with widowhood. In 2022, she published "Old Rage," and in 2014, she released her debut novel titled "Miss Carter's War." Hancock had previously published her memoir, "Ramblings of an Actress," in 1987.

Hancock is a member of the Religious Society of Friends, also known as Quakers. She is involved in charitable work and serves as a patron of the educational charity Digismart. Additionally, she is a trustee of the John Thaw Foundation, which supports young actors.

In recognition of her contributions to drama and charity, Hancock has received several honors. She was appointed Officer of the Order of the British Empire (OBE) in the 1974 Birthday Honours, Commander of the Order of the British Empire (CBE) in the 2011 New Year Honours, and Dame Commander of the Order of the British Empire (DBE) in the 2021 New Year Honours.

Hancock is known to be a friend of Sandi Toksvig, a fellow comedian and broadcaster. She also participated in an event called "I Do To Equal Marriage," where she read Maya Angelou's poem "Touched by an Angel" to celebrate the introduction of same-sex marriage in England and Wales.

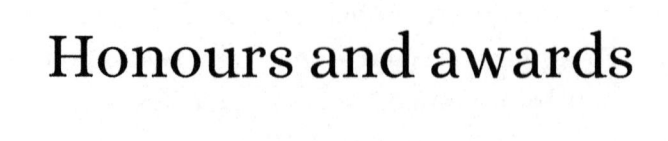

Honours and awards

Sheila Hancock has received numerous honours and awards throughout her career in recognition of her talent and contributions to the world of drama. Some of her notable honours and awards include:

1966 Tony Award nomination for Best Actress in a Play for her performance in "Entertaining Mr Sloane."
1974 Officer of the Order of the British Empire (OBE) for her services to drama.
1978 Laurence Olivier Award nomination for Best Comedy Performance for her portrayal of Miss Hannigan in "Annie."
1980 Laurence Olivier Award nomination for Best Actress in a Musical for her role as Mrs Lovett in "Sweeney Todd."
1982 Laurence Olivier Award nomination for Best Supporting Actress for her performance as Paulina in "The Winter's Tale."
1989 Laurence Olivier Award nomination for Best Actress for her role as Prin in "Prin."
2002 BAFTA nomination for Best Actress for her work in "The Russian Bride."
2003 BAFTA nomination for Best Actress for her role in "Bedtime."
In 2007, she was appointed as the Chancellor of the University of Portsmouth.
2007 Laurence Olivier Award for Best Performance in a Supporting Role in a Musical for her portrayal of Fraulein Schneider in "Cabaret."
2010 Laurence Olivier Award nomination for Best Performance in a Supporting Role in a Musical for her role as Mother Superior in "Sister Act the Musical."
In 2010, she received the Lifetime Achievement Award at the Women in Film and Television Awards.

2011 Commander of the Order of the British Empire (CBE) for her services to drama.

In 2021, she was honored as Dame Commander of the Order of the British Empire (DBE) for her contributions to drama and charity.

These awards and honours highlight Sheila Hancock's outstanding achievements and her significant impact in the field of drama.

Filmography

Here is Sheila Hancock's filmography:

1960: "Light Up the Sky!" (Theatre Act)
1960: "The Bulldog Breed" (Doris) - Uncredited
1960: "Doctor in Love" (Librarian) - Uncredited
1961: "The Girl on the Boat" (Jane Hubbard)
1962: "Twice Round the Daffodils" (Dora)
1964: "Night Must Fall" (Dora Parkoe)
1964: "The Moon-Spinners" (Cynthia Gamble)
1964: "Carry On Cleo" (Senna Pod)
1967: "How I Won the War" (Mrs. Clapper's Friend)
1968: "The Anniversary" (Karen Taggart)
1970: "Take a Girl Like You" (Martha Thompson)
1980: "The Wildcats of St Trinian's" (Olga Vandemeer)
1987: "Making Waves" (Doris) - Short film
1988: "Hawks" (Regina)
1988: "Buster" (Mrs. Rothery)
1988: "The Universe of Dermot Finn" (Mother of Pearl) - Short film
1990: "Three Men and a Little Lady" (Vera)
1994: "A Business Affair" (Judith)
1997: "Love and Death on Long Island" (Mrs. Barker)
1999: "Hold Back the Night" (Vera)
2004: "Yes" (Aunt)
2008: "The Boy in the Striped Pyjamas" (Grandma)
2013: "Delicious" (Patti)
2017: "Edie" (Edie)
2017: "The Dark Mile" (Mary)
2018: "The More You Ignore Me" (Nan Wildgoose)
2019: "From This Day Forward" (Her) - Short film

Here is a partial list of Sheila Hancock's television credits:

1960: "Bootsie and Snudge" (Greta) - Episode: "Bootsie's Punctured Romance"
1960: "BBC Sunday-Night Play" (Janet) - Episode: "Twentieth Century Theatre: Doctor in the House"
1961-62: "The Rag Trade" (Carole Taylor) - 12 episodes
1963: "BBC Sunday-Night Play" (Jackie Lambert) - Episode: "June Fall"
1964: "Festival" (Winifred) - Episode: "Say Nothing"
1964: "Thursday Theatre" (Olive Leech) - Episode: "Summer of the Seventeenth Doll"
1965: "ITV Play of the Week" (Hety) - Episode: "A Fearful Thing"
1965: "The Wednesday Thriller" (Joyce Lambert) - Episode: "The Regulator"
1966: "The Bed-Sit Girl" (Sheila Ross) - 12 episodes
1966-81: "Jackanory" (Storyteller) - 15 episodes
1967: "Armchair Theatre" (Alice) - Episode: "Compensation Alice"
1967: "Life with Cooper" (Lady Stuck In Railings) - 1 episode
1968: "ITV Playhouse" (Naomi Woodley) - Episode: "Horizontal Hold"
1968: "Kaff" - Episode: "Entertaining Mr Sloane"
1968: "Release" (Mrs Caudle) - Episode: "Mrs. Caudle's Curtain Lectures"
1968: "Detective" (Mrs Markle) - Episode: "Born Victim"
1969: "All Star Comedy Carnival" (Thelma Teesdale)
1969-71: "Mr Digby Darling" (Thelma Teesdale) - 19 episodes
1970: "The Mating Machine" (Freda) - Episode: "Sealed with a Loving Kiss"
1970: "Comedy Playhouse" (Wendy Hillbright) - Episode: "Better Than a Man"
1971: "Claire Love" - Episode: "Just Harry and Me"
1971: "Shadows of Fear" (Anne Brand) - Episode: "Sugar and Spice"
1971: "Now Take My Wife" (Claire Love) - 14 episodes
1972: "Scoop" (Mrs Stitch) - 3 episodes
1976: "Whodunnit?" (Panellist) - Episode: "Dead Grass"
1982: "Play for Today" (Ellen) - Episode: "The Remainder Man"
1985: "Dramarama" (Rita Chartell) - Episode: "The Audition"
1985: "The Daughter-in-Law" (Mrs Gascoigne)
1988: "Doctor Who" (Helen A.) - Episode: "The Happiness Patrol"
1989: "Theatre Night" (Mrs Malaprop) - Episode: "The Rivals"

1985: "The Daughter-in-Law" (Mrs Gascoigne)
1988: "Doctor Who" (Helen A.) - Episode: "The Happiness Patrol"
1989: "Theatre Night" (Mrs Malaprop) - Episode: "The Rivals"
1991: "Gone to the Dogs" (Jean) - 4 episodes
1993: "Comedy Playhouse" (Frances) - Episode: "Brighton Belles: Pilot"
1993-94: "The Brighton Belles" (Frances) - 11 episodes
1995: "Dangerous Lady" (Sarah Ryan)
1999: "Alice in Wonderland" (Cook) - TV movie
2000-01: "EastEnders" (Barbara) - 3 episodes
2003: "Bedtime" (Alice Oldfield) - 15 episodes
2005: "Bleak House" (Mrs Guppy)
2006: "The Catherine Tate Show" (Auntie June) - Season 3, Episode 6
2009: "Moving On" (Liz) - Episode: "The Rain Has Stopped"
2016-19: "Delicious" (Mimi Vincent) - 12 episodes
2017: "Endeavour" (Dowsable Chattox) - Episode: "Harvest"
2021: "A Discovery of Witches" (Goody Alsop) - 5 episodes
2021: "Unforgotten" (Eileen Baildon) - 4 episodes

Printed in Great Britain
by Amazon